Army Medical Department Transformation

Executive Summary of Five Workshops

David E. Johnson, Gary Cecchine, Jerry M. Sollinger

Prepared for the United States Army

Approved for public release; distribution unlimited

 ARROYO CENTER and RAND HEALTH

The research described in this report was sponsored by the United States Army under Contract No. DASW01-01-C-0003.

Library of Congress Cataloging-in-Publication Data

Johnson, David E., 1950 Oct. 16–
    Army Medical Department transformation : a summary of five workshops /
David E. Johnson, Gary Cecchine, Jerry M. Sollinger.
        p. cm.
    "MG-416."
    Includes bibliographical references.
    ISBN 0-8330-3906-7 (pbk.)
    1. United States. Army—Medical care. 2. United States. Army Medical Dept.
3. United States. Army—Reorganization. I. Cecchine, Gary. II. Sollinger, Jerry M.
III. Rand Corporation. IV. United States. Army Medical Dept. V. Title.
    [DNLM: 1. United States. Army Medical Dept. 2. Military Medicine—
organization & administration. 3. Military Science—methods. 4. Computer
Simulation. 5. Models, Logistical. WB 116 J66a 2006]

UH223.J635 2006
355.3'450973—dc22

                                                                    2005036285

The RAND Corporation is a nonprofit research organization providing objective analysis and effective solutions that address the challenges facing the public and private sectors around the world. RAND's publications do not necessarily reflect the opinions of its research clients and sponsors.

RAND® is a registered trademark.

Published 2006 by the RAND Corporation
1776 Main Street, P.O. Box 2138, Santa Monica, CA 90407-2138
1200 South Hayes Street, Arlington, VA 22202-5050
201 North Craig Street, Suite 202, Pittsburgh, PA 15213-1516
RAND URL: http://www.rand.org/
To order RAND documents or to obtain additional information, contact
Distribution Services: Telephone: (310) 451-7002;
Fax: (310) 451-6915; Email: order@rand.org

Preface

This report summarizes a series of five Army Medical Command Transformational Workshops that were held between 2002 and 2004. The purpose of these workshops was to assess the effect of Future Force doctrine on the ability of the Health Service Support system to deliver medical care on the battlefield and to identify medical issues in the Army's transformation efforts. The Army Medical Command began an analytic effort in 1998 to gain insight into the challenges that emerging Army concepts would pose for it, conducting a series of games and workshops. This work provided the basis for a series of scenario-based workshops that assessed the medical risks associated with emerging concepts and the Army Medical Command's ability to mitigate that risk. This summary is based on RAND Arroyo Center reports about the individual workshops. These reports include the following:

- David E. Johnson and Gary Cecchine, *Conserving the Future Force Fighting Strength: Findings from the Army Medical Department Transformation Workshops,* MG-103-A, 2004.
- David E. Johnson and Gary Cecchine, *Medical Risk in the Future Force Unit of Action: Results of the Army Medical Department Transformation Workshop IV,* TR-253-A, 2005.
- David E. Johnson and Gary Cecchine, *Medical Risk in the Future Force Unit of Employment: Results of the Army Medical Department Transformation Workshop V,* TR-302-A, forthcoming.

These studies will interest those involved with Future Force doctrine and structure and those concerned with the delivery of battlefield medical care.

The Commanding General, U.S. Army Medical Department Center and School, sponsored this work, which was carried out jointly by RAND Arroyo Center's Manpower and Training Program and RAND Health's Center for Military Health Policy Research. RAND Arroyo Center, part of the RAND Corporation, is a federally funded research and development center sponsored by the U.S. Army.

For more information on RAND Arroyo Center, contact the Director of Operations (telephone 310-393-0411, extension 6419; FAX 310-451-6952; email Marcy_Agmon@rand.org), or visit Arroyo's web site at http://www.rand.org/ard/.

Contents

Figures

Tables

Summary

Background and Purpose

The Army has been transforming itself into what it calls the Future Force, which relies on a combination of rapid operations, dispersed forces, and superior information to enable a medium-weight force to fight with the punch of heavy conventional forces. These new concepts pose considerable challenges for the organizations that support the combat forces on the battlefield, and the challenge is particularly great for medical forces, which must find, stabilize, and evacuate casualties that are spread across a dispersed battlefield. To determine what the new concepts mean for providing medical support to the fighting units, the Army Medical Department (AMEDD) conducted five Transformation Workshops (ATWs) from 2002 to 2004 to identify the challenges the new concepts posed to providing battlefield medical support and to explore what those challenges might imply for medical force structure.

The workshops all employed a technique based on *"The Day After . . ."* format, which was developed at the RAND Corporation as a way of dealing with issues related to nuclear proliferation policy. The workshops used data provided to their designers by the U.S. Army Training and Doctrine Command (TRADOC) Analysis Center (TRAC) drawn from approved Army scenarios and simulations to generate casualties, which were then tracked independently by teams of subject matter experts. Scenarios and simulations used appear in Table S.1. We note that the small number of scenarios and simula-

Table S.1
Scenarios and Simulations Used in the ATWs

Workshop	Scenario	Simulation
ATWs I and III	Objective Force Concept of Operation: A Notional Combat Battalion Engagement (TRAD-F-TC-01-006)	Interactive Distributed Engineering Evaluation and Analysis Simulation (IDEEAS)
ATW IV	Caspian 2.0 scenario[a]	JANUS
ATW V	Caspian 2.0 scenario[a]	Vector in Command (VIC)

[a] This scenario is approved by the Defense Planning Guidance.

tions used constitute an important methodological limitation and that the insights derived from the workshops are sensitive to this limitation. The scenarios determined the force structure, equipment, how forces were arrayed on the battlefield, and so forth, and the simulations determined the number and nature of combat results (vehicles destroyed or damaged, individuals killed or wounded). The subject matter experts then converted the nature of the kill (e.g., catastrophic kill[1]) into specific medical conditions.[2] Casualties were then tracked through the Health Service Support (HSS) system posited for the scenario.

The purpose of tracking the individual casualties was to see what happened to the HSS system set up as part of the workshop to treat the casualties. The first three workshops largely were a baseline effort that focused on a battalion-sized Unit of Action (UA) that fought for eight hours. They were a baseline effort in the sense that they validated the methodology and procedures, the composition of the teams of subject matter experts, and the casualty tracking process. Subsequent workshops employed the methodologies and procedures of the

---

[1] A catastrophic kill renders a vehicle both unusable and unrepairable. Typically a catastrophic kill ignites any fuel the vehicle may be carrying and detonates its ammunition. It does not preclude the survival of the vehicle's crew.

[2] The wound conditions were described by treatment briefs that were specific enough to enable the subject matter experts to make judgments about evacuation and treatment, e.g., "wound, face and neck, open, lacerated, contused without fractures, severe, with airway obstructions and/or major vessel involvement."

first three. The ensuing workshops considered larger UAs (brigade size), longer battles, and larger battlefields. The overarching purpose of the workshops was to answer two questions. First, what medical risk do Army Future Force operations pose? Second, what can the AMEDD do to mitigate that risk? The HSS system posited in the workshops was the one designed to support units like those employed in the scenarios, except that it was comparatively generous for the first three workshops and it did not degrade during the scenarios. That is, neither personnel nor equipment became a combat loss. The medical structure available to treat the wounded was designed to be a best case. Thus, the ATW outcomes would represent the best performance the HSS system can be expected to deliver for scenarios like the ones used here.

Results and Implications

Although the workshops used different scenarios and simulations, the results were remarkably consistent. Below we summarize the conclusions and the most significant issues that emerged from the five workshops.

Based on the data gathered during the five workshops, RAND analysts concluded that the distances envisioned for the Future Force battlefield present knotty problems for medical support. The dispersion creates a situation in which it will be unlikely that a medic will be nearby when a soldier is wounded and in which ground evacuation of casualties will be difficult. Given the challenges posed by these scenarios, it also appears that the medical echelons above the UA could expect a substantial patient load. Finally, the analysts concluded that better simulations are needed to help the AMEDD explore questions of medical force structure in more detail.

Significant issues included the following.

Combat Lifesavers and Combat Medics

Fast-paced operations on a dispersed battlefield make it difficult to provide a soldier immediate medical care when wounded because a combat medic may not be nearby. In the scenarios for the ATWs, typical distances between a combat medic and a wounded soldier were a kilometer or greater. The AMEDD dealt with this problem by imbuing the combat lifesavers—combat soldiers with additional training in medical skills—with a high level of medical skill, seen by some players as approaching those of a combat medic. The subject matter experts who participated in the workshops were skeptical that combat soldiers could be trained to the level suggested by the scenario, or, if they could be trained that well, the experts doubted that such skills could be sustained.

After reviewing the outputs of the five workshops, RAND Arroyo Center researchers concluded that the most straightforward options all carry major drawbacks. The Army could accept the fact that the first responders would be combat lifesavers and train them to near-medic levels. This approach would present a substantial training challenge (it takes 16 weeks to train a combat medic as opposed to three days for a combat lifesaver), as would sustaining these skills, which tend to atrophy quickly without frequent hands-on practice. Even if the additional training for a combat lifesaver did not take as long as that of a combat medic, the extra skills would still be an additional training burden, which would inevitably compete with a soldier's proficiency in his primary military skill. Alternatively, the Army could choose to increase the number of combat medics in the UA. This step would have force structure, recruiting, and training implications. Or the Army could modify its doctrine and operate with units closer together. While this might get a wounded soldier medical care faster, it might also increase the vulnerability of units and would require the Army to accept a major change to its Future Force doctrine. Finally, the Army could simply choose to accept the medical risk created by the current HSS structure and dispersed operations. Based on the results of the workshops, the potential consequence of this decision would be seriously wounded soldiers dying or not receiving timely medical attention.

Surgical Force Structure and Evacuation Capabilities

Even if the Army and AMEDD managed to provide skilled first responders, they would still have to deal with the casualty treatment problem. The first responder simply stabilizes a wounded soldier so that he can be evacuated to a surgical treatment facility. But the workshops showed that, given the scenarios and simulations used, the forward surgical teams were at or near full capacity, especially the surgical capability. The subject matter experts who participated in the workshops carefully managed the surgical queue, ensuring that the most severely wounded soldiers got treatment first. But this meant that other wounded had to wait for surgery, and this might explain the increased number of patients who lost limbs. Even with this careful management, the time between injury and treatment averaged between 2.7 hours in ATW IV and 7.5 hours in ATW V. Medical outcomes often can be expected to get worse as the time to initial surgical treatment lengthens, but this project did not determine the likely effects of the treatment delays or identify maximum treatment delay standards for different types of patients. In the last two workshops, surgery could be performed in the UA or casualties could be stabilized and transported to higher echelons for surgery. The results of ATWs IV and V indicate that the UA's residual load of casualties requiring surgery and additional treatment will create a heavy demand for an echelons-above-UA HSS system. Of course, some of these casualties could be evacuated to the medical facilities of other services if available.

Again, RAND researchers analyzing the results of the five workshops conclude that the straightforward options for ensuring appropriately prompt treatment for all patients also carry drawbacks. The Army and AMEDD could opt to increase the surgical capacity of the UA, either by adding more forward surgical teams or by increasing the capability of the current teams by adding more personnel and equipment. Either choice would have important force structure implications. Alternatively, the Army could decide to increase the air evacuation capabilities in the UA, although some patients would still require surgical stabilization before being shipped. The medevac helicopters available during the workshop scenarios were typically used to capacity, so if the decision were to ship casualties outside of the UA, more medevac helicopters would have to be provided. This assumes that the evacuation distances are not too great. If the distances approach hundreds of kilometers, as they did at times during the workshops, the problem remains.

Advanced Technologies

Throughout the five workshops, participants had 21 advanced medical technologies available to treat battlefield casualties. The purpose of the workshop was not to evaluate these technologies individually, but analysis of workshop results show that two were especially important: the Warfighter Physiological Status Monitor (WPSM), a networked array of physiological monitors embedded in a soldier's combat uniform, and advanced hemostatic agents such as spray-on bandages and hemostatic drugs that enhance the body's natural clotting function. The WPSM provided critical location information, enabled remote triage, and facilitated allocation of evacuation assets. The hemostatic agents helped control bleeding, which prevented fatal hemorrhage while severely wounded casualties were en route to treatment at the forward surgical team. This was important given the evacuation distances. The implication is that had these two technologies not been available, the medical outcomes of the workshops would have been decidedly worse than described here.

Army-Level Issues

Two issues cropped up during the workshops that fall outside the Army Medical Command's purview but are important enough to warrant attention from the Army. One has to do with unsecured lines of communication. As the battle progressed, the lines of communication lengthened steadily and were largely unsecured as the combat units pressed on to their objectives. The forward surgical teams had so many casualties to deal with that they could not displace forward to keep pace with the maneuver units. The upshot of this situation was that ground medical evacuation vehicles had to move independently to casualty locations, casualty collection points, aerial medical evacuation landing zones, and so forth, across a battlefield that was neither cleared nor secured. This implies that the forward surgical team and casualty collectors would require additional security.

A second issue involves unit cohesion and morale. As we pointed out above, the workshops showed that it was difficult for a combat medic to reach a casualty, and combat lifesavers had to plug the gap. In past contingencies, when a wounded soldier needed a medic, one appeared. Furthermore, in the scenarios the distance between the place where a soldier was wounded and where he received surgical care gradually lengthened, with the result that it took longer and longer to get soldiers to a forward surgical team. This situation would reverse the historical trend, which began in Korea when the Army started using helicopters to evacuate soldiers rapidly: The time from sustaining a wound to arrival in surgery has generally gone down. The dispersion called for in the Future Force doctrine causes the time from becoming wounded to arriving in surgery to lengthen. These two factors—(1) either no available medics or ones who arrive after a substantial delay and (2) lengthening evacuation times over the course of battle—could contribute to feelings of being abandoned and adversely affect morale.

In sum, then, the workshops showed that a robust HSS system that did not lose any of its capability during the battles was at or near its capacity in the scenarios employing the Future Force structure. This state of being at capacity occurred despite some highly favorable (and some would argue unrealistic) assumptions about the level of care provided by the first responder and the availability and effectiveness of advanced medical technologies. Ensuring that all patients are treated within an appropriate timeframe may pose challenges, because all options carry unwelcome aspects. But the Army must either accept some force structure, training, or doctrinal changes, or be willing to assume a degree of medical risk that it has been unwilling to bear in the past.

Abbreviations

AMEDD	Army Medical Department
AMEDD C&S	Army Medical Department Center and School
ATW	AMEDD Transformation Workshop
CSH	Combat Support Hospital
DOW	Died of wounds
FCS	Future Combat System
FST	Forward Surgical Team
HSS	Health Service Support
ICU	Intensive care unit
IDEEAS	Interactive Distributed Engineering Evaluation and Analysis Simulation
KIA	Killed in action
OR	Operating room
MRMC	Medical Research and Materiel Command
RTD	Returned to duty
TRAC	[U.S. Army] Training and Doctrine Command (TRADOC) Analysis Center
TRADOC	Training and Doctrine Command
UA	Unit of Action
UE	Unit of Employment
VIC	Vector in Command

WIA   Wounded in action
WPSM   Warfighter Physiological Status Monitor

CHAPTER ONE

Introduction

Background

All of the military services are in the process of transforming, moving away from force organizations and operational concepts of the Cold War to ones better suited to the security threats the United States faces today. The Army, arguably, is undertaking the most sweeping transformation of any of the services. Not only is it attempting to field radically different equipment, but also it is planning on fighting in different ways. One hallmark of the new operational concepts contemplated by the Army is forces that are carrying out fast-paced operations and that are spread widely across a battlefield devoid of the linear boundaries that characterized most past operations.

The concept of fast-paced operations on a dispersed battlefield poses substantial problems for the units that support the combat forces. Medical units face challenges that are greater than those of most other support units. Finding casualties quickly, treating them promptly, and evacuating them rapidly will be difficult. But each of these tasks will be crucial to keeping mortality and morbidity low.

In 1998, the Army Medical Department (AMEDD) started an analytic process to identify the specific challenges these new concepts will pose to providing Health Service Support (HSS). To do so, the AMEDD conducted war games and workshops. These efforts resulted in a list of issues to be rank ordered by a council of colonels. Researchers from RAND were asked to comment on and assess the proceedings and the conclusions.

The researchers determined that the issues identified by the AMEDD process fell into two categories: the level of medical risk posed and the AMEDD's role in mitigating that risk. Medical risk refers to the potential casualties—including soldiers, enemy prisoners of war, and civilians—and their outcomes.

RAND researchers suggested that the AMEDD take the approach of scenario planning, which is a strategic management tool that assumes a largely unknowable future. It is a group process that attempts to learn about the future by understanding the most important influences affecting it. The goal is to consider as many perspectives as possible. In that sense, it is the polar opposite of a view that assumes a specific future outcome and identifies the steps along the way to reach that specific end.

The AMEDD accepted this recommendation and asked its researchers to design a series of AMEDD Transformation Workshops (ATWs) to begin an assessment of the medical risks associated with the emerging Army operational concepts and the capability of the HSS system to mitigate them. The underlying goal was to identify the gaps between the HSS concepts for the Future Force and the requirements for that force, and to gauge the medical risk those gaps pose. Figure 1.1 depicts the general process used in these workshops.

Each workshop employed a combat simulation that produced results in terms of soldiers and vehicles being struck by enemy weapons. Workshop participants then used a process to determine what those combat results meant in terms of casualties, to include the type of casualty and when and where it occurred. Teams of subject matter experts, informed by the assumptions made about the HSS system, then took the casualty data and deliberated on what type of treatment and evacuation was required and feasible at each stage of a casualty's progress through the HSS system, from treatment by the first responder through the forward surgical teams and UA medical companies.

The results and implications of these workshops depend in important ways on the scenarios and the models. First, the small num-

Figure 1.1
ATW Process

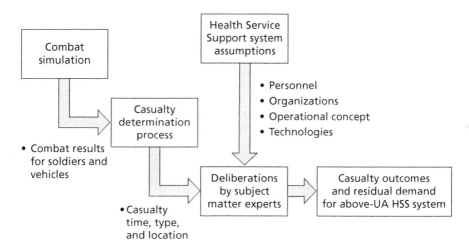

ber of scenarios examined and the limited number of models used impose a significant methodological limitation, and the insights derived are sensitive to it. Second, the workshops employed a relatively sophisticated array of analytic assets to track the flow of patients through the HSS system. Clearly, the results depend heavily on particular features of this layered approach. For example, the number of casualties depended in part on the combat outcomes of the combat models and on data about casualty distribution drawn from the historical literature. Table 1.1 lays out these dependencies. Future attempts to refine the analysis of these issues should take these dependencies into account.

Purpose

Between April 2002 and May 2004, the AMEDD conducted five workshops. This report briefly describes the scenarios, structure, and processes of the workshops. However, its main purpose is to summa-

Table 1.1
Scenario and Model Dependencies

Results/Observations	Assumptions/Data Elements on Which Conclusions Depend			
	Battlefield Size in Scenario	High Resolution Combat Model	Historical Casualty Rates	Subject Matter Expert Case Judgment Based on ATW Worksheets
Time to recover casualties	√	√		
Mounted (in vehicles) and dismounted (on foot) casualties		√		
Number and type of wounds sustained		√	√	
Treatment regimes				√
Time required to treat individual patients				√
Time required to treat patients in queues	√	√	√	√

NOTE: These workshops focused on combat casualties. They did not deal with injuries caused by accidents or disease, nor did they consider enemy or noncombatant injuries.

rize their results. Workshop output included the responses by teams of subject matter experts to a series of questions and issues raised by the workshops. In most cases, several workshops addressed the same issues and questions, albeit from the different perspectives imposed by the specific scenario. Output also included the broader implications of the workshops. Some of these pertain to the HSS system; others transcend that system and apply to the Army as a whole.

How the Report Is Organized

The next chapter describes the five workshops. The one following that presents the subject matter expert perspectives from the workshops on the issues and questions they addressed. The final chapter describes the broader implications of the workshops. Appendix A contains a list of the subject matter experts. Appendix B lists the advanced medical technologies that the scenario uses.

CHAPTER TWO

The Workshops

The AMEDD and RAND completed five individual workshops. ATWs I–III were conducted in April, August, and November of 2002, respectively. ATW IV occurred in February 2004, and ATV V took place in May 2004. The general structure of the workshops was the same. Each involved a combat scenario lasting between 8 and 100 hours and teams of subject matter experts whose areas of expertise spanned the functional areas critical to an analysis of combat casualty care issues. The simulations used varied across the workshops, but the general procedure was to assess the number and types of casualties that were incurred during the simulated combat and to track those casualties through the HSS system. Each workshop addressed a number of issues and questions. Many of these overlapped several workshops, but some issues were examined in solitary workshops.

The following were the broad purposes of all the workshops:

- Identify gaps between AMEDD Future Force HSS system concepts and combat casualty care requirements generated from simulations sponsored by the U.S. Army Training and Doctrine Command (TRADOC) Analysis Center (TRAC).
- Identify potential solutions and alternatives for further analysis.
- Provide the AMEDD analytic support for programmatic decisions.
- Assess the medical risks and the potential to mitigate them.

Although all workshops had the same overarching objectives, each had different specific objectives. The workshops also employed different HSS structures, different simulation tools, and focused on different echelons. Table 2.1 compares the workshops across several dimensions.

ATWs I and II

The first three workshops were considered baseline efforts in the sense that they validated the methodology, procedures, and composition of the teams of subject matter experts. The judgment of the workshop participants was that the methodology and procedures were valid. While baseline, they also provided some insight into HSS system capabilities. Three small teams of subject matter experts each containing ten members supported these workshops. The subject matter experts were mostly officers and noncommissioned officers of the AMEDD, and their skills included aerial evacuation, medical doctrine, ground evacuation, anesthesiology, combat medic, medical technology, trauma, and general surgery. A list of these experts appears in Appendix A. The scenario for the first two workshops involved a Unit of Action (UA) battalion operating in 2015 as part of a brigade involved in a shaping operation that lasted eight hours. The teams independently considered each casualty as he moved through the HSS system, determining what type of treatment and evacuation were required and what could be provided given the assets available in the scenario. The specific objectives were as follows:

- Design an analytic architecture to evaluate HSS system concepts by assessing AMEDD issues.
- Identify gaps between Army and AMEDD concepts and capabilities and HSS requirements derived from Future Force operational scenarios.
- Begin to identify and assess alternative HSS system concepts.

Table 2.1
Summary of ATWs

Dimension	I	II	III	IV	V
Date	April 2002	August 2002	November 2002	February 2004	May 2004
Scenario timeframe	2015	2015	2015	2015	2015
Nature of battle	Blue UA battalion attacks Red brigade	Blue UA battalion attacks Red brigade	Blue UA battalion attacks Red brigade	Blue augmented UA battalion attacks 12 brigades	Blue UE and 4 UAs battalions attack 3 Red corps
Length of battle	8 hours	8 hours	8 hours	12 hours	> 100 hours
Size of battlefield	80 km x 80 km	80 km x 80 km	80 km x 80 km	75 km x 85 km	500 km x 225 km
Simulation	IDEEAS	IDEEAS	IDEEAS	JANUS	VIC
Scenario	TRAC notional combat battalion engagement on Balkans 2.0 terrain	TRAC notional combat battalion engagement on Balkans 2.0 terrain	TRAC notional combat battalion engagement on Balkans 2.0 terrain	Caspian 2.0	Caspian 2.0
Nature of HSS simulated	UA + 44 bed CSH	ATW I with less capable HSS	ATW I with reorganized HSS	UA HSS with evacuation	UE HSS with evacuation
Portion of HSS simulated	Wound through CSH	Wound through CSH	Wound through CSH	Wound through FST, evacuation above UA	Wound through FST, evacuation above UA
Number of casualties assessed	54	54	54	76	429
Number of subject matter expert assessments per casualty	3	3	3	2	1

NOTES: UA = Unit of Action; UE = Unit of Employment; IDEEAS = Interactive Distributed Engineering Evaluation and Analysis Simulation; VIC = Vector in Command; CHS = Combat Support Hospital; FST = Forward Surgical Team.

HSS System Employed in Workshops

Generally, the HSS structure used in the workshops was the one designed for units similar to those used in the scenario, except for ATWs I–III, where the structure was relatively generous given the size of the unit. The workshop employed a three-tier HSS system: first responders, a single UA's medical assets, and elements of division-level assets.

The first responder was either a combat medic (Military Occupational Skill 91W), a combat lifesaver, or the individual solider. A combat medic has skills similar to those of an emergency medical technician found on civilian ambulances. Combat medic skills focus on emergency care such as restoring breathing, stopping bleeding and shock, and evacuation. A combat lifesaver is a combat soldier who has received some additional medical training.[1] Individual soldiers also receive training in self-aid.

The UA battalion headquarters had 14 evacuation vehicles, 12 of which were attached to maneuver companies (two each) and two attached to the Reconnaissance, Surveillance, and Target Acquisition squadron. The brigade headquarters had a medical company (20 minimal care beds) and aerial evacuation provided by a forward support medevac team (three UH-60L helicopters). The Forward Surgical Team (FST) is a light medical unit that deploys operating room capabilities forward in the battle area to save the lives of those whose injuries are so serious that they would not live to reach a rear area hospital. It can staff two operating tables. Medical personnel include four surgeons; eight nurses with critical care, anesthesiology, operating room, medical surgical, and practical nursing skills; and six enlisted personnel involved in patient care. The FST can handle about 10 patients per day or 30 in 72 hours (U.S. Department of the Army, 1997, pp. 2-1–2-7). After that time, the supplies and personnel are

---

[1] Combat lifesavers receive medical training beyond what a typical soldier receives. The training lasts three days, and a combat lifesaver must be recertified annually. Skills taught are "buddy aid" (clear object from mouth of conscious patient, apply field dressing, pressure dressing, and tourniquet) and two medical tasks (initiate intravenous infusion and monitor a casualty's pulse). The goal is to have one member of each squad, crew, or like-sized element as a combat lifesaver (U.S. Department of the Army, 1995, p. 17).

both exhausted. Furthermore, any soldier treated at the FST will likely also require treatment at the next higher medical echelon. By doctrine, an FST typically supports a combat brigade.

A full Combat Support Hospital (CSH), typically assigned to echelons above the UA, contains 236 beds: 36 intensive, 140 intermediate, 40 minimal, and 20 neuropsychiatric care (U.S. Department of the Army, 2005, pp. 2-1–2-22). It has two operating room (OR) modules, one surgical and the other orthopedic, which are staffed to provide a total of 96 OR table hours per day. It also allows for attachment of specialty surgical teams. It is an independent organization that includes all hospital services.

The workshops did not use a full-sized CSH. Rather they employed a 44-bed module (24 intensive care beds and 20 intermediate care) that included one surgical OR module. This module provides general surgical services with two OR tables for a total of 36 hours of table time per day. It can do more complex surgeries and has greater specialized capabilities (such as intensive care) than the FST, but its capacity in terms of numbers is about the same. The staff is composed of general surgeons, OR nurses, nurse anesthetists, and OR specialists. In the workshop, the CSH was located at the airport where the troops disembarked.

The only *organic* medical assistance available at platoon level was highly trained combat lifesavers, i.e., combat soldiers who had additional training in lifesaving techniques. In ATW I, a medic was attached to each platoon, and the UA battalion had two evacuation vehicles for each company-sized unit and three treatment/evacuation vehicles, which were all variants of the Future Combat System vehicle. In ATW II, the UA battalion was reduced to one evacuation vehicle for each company and two treatment/evacuation vehicles. No medics were attached to the platoons. No medical assets were degraded during the operation—i.e., no medics became casualties and no helicopters got shot down; command, control, communications, computer, intelligence, surveillance, and reconnaissance systems worked flawlessly and medical materiel was unrestricted. The medical units used in the workshop were the ones that exist in the Army today.

Overall, the scenario posited a relatively generous medical structure to support the theater and did not hold any parts of that structure at risk. Typically, an FST supports a full brigade, whereas in this scenario only a UA battalion (roughly one-third the size of a brigade-sized UA) was involved in the fight. Normally, a CSH would support an echelon above the brigade, either a division or a Unit of Employment, which typically have three combat brigades or UAs. But since only one UA was involved in the scenario, the full assets of the 44-bed CSH module were available to it. Casualties were sent to whichever facility had available capacity.

How the Workshops Determined Casualties

Each workshop involved a scenario and a simulation. The scenario for ATWs I–III was developed by TRADOC (U.S. Department of the Army, TRAC, 2001). It involved a UA battalion consisting of six combined arms companies operating in an 80-square kilometer area in southwestern Kosovo. The terrain was a mix of complex geography including forests and cities. The scenario called for the UA battalion to attack an enemy brigade in well-established defensive positions in forested terrain as part of a shaping operation. The threat was equipped commensurately with capabilities projected to be available in 2015. The battalion, with its reconnaissance element in the lead, made a 60-kilometer advance while attacking the enemy with long-range fires. Once it reached the enemy's position, the battalion assumed tactical standoff positions and continued to attack threat forces with fires to set the conditions for a close assault. When the destruction criterion was met, five of the six companies assaulted the enemy position to seize, clear, and secure the terrain. The battle lasted eight hours.

The TRAC at Fort Leavenworth used a standard Army simulation, the Interactive Distributed Engineering Evaluation and Analysis Simulation (IDEEAS), to produce a list of all friendly personnel or vehicles struck by enemy fire. IDEEAS is a high-fidelity engineering-level simulation loaded with over 1,700 entities to represent the UA battalion and the opposing threat, a brigade-sized mechanized unit.

The simulation determined which friendly elements were hit and assigned each to one of five categories: catastrophic kill, mobility damage, firepower damage, mobility and firepower damage, and crew kill (i.e., the number killed or disabled is greater than the minimum number of soldiers required to operate a towed vehicle). The simulation also provided the severity of the damage when a friendly element was hit, e.g., a catastrophic and combined firepower and mobility kill yield a 0.2 probability of a crewmember being killed and a 0.5 probability of being wounded. A catastrophic kill of a dismounted soldier yields a 1.0 probability that the soldier is killed.

The AMEDD Center and School (C&S) used a methodical process to determine how many soldiers were wounded as a result of being struck by enemy fire and to assign each one a discrete patient condition for the subject matter expert teams to manage. As described above, the process began with a battle damage assessment category above, as determined by the supporting simulation. The AMEDD C&S then applied a historically derived probability to the dismounted soldier, crew member, or platform occupant to determine if an individual was killed in action (KIA),[2] wounded in action (WIA), or not injured. Once the number of wounded was determined, each casualty was then randomly assigned a patient condition code based on a frequency distribution from the Patient Workload Generator Model used by the AMEDD C&S.

After the nature of the wound was determined, each casualty was entered into a tracking worksheet, which detailed the type of weapon that caused the casualty, whether the casualty was in a vehicle or dismounted, the scenario time of the wounding, a location, the wound type, and standard for treatment. The worksheet was turned

---

[2] The term KIA can have different meanings. One refers to a soldier who is killed outright when struck by enemy fire. Such a soldier never enters the medical treatment system. The medical community has a different meaning. To it, a KIA refers to a casualty who dies after entering the medical system but before receiving effective medical care—i.e., before being treated at a medical treatment facility. More specifically, it means dying before reaching the battalion aid station. Thus, the number of medical KIA will differ from and be less than the number of overall KIA for a given battle. This narrower definition complicates comparisons across conflicts, which typically report a single figure for KIA. A casualty who dies after reaching a medical treatment facility is classified as "died of wounds" (DOW).

over to each of the expert panels. Each panel then independently de-cided what medical treatment the patient needed to receive and in what location.

Other Scenario Attributes

The scenario also employed advanced medical technologies expected to be available by 2015. These included such things as the Warfighter Physiological Status Monitor (WPSM), which is a networked array of physiological monitors embedded in a soldier's combat uniform; spray-on bandages; and hemostatic drugs that enhance the body's natural clotting function. Twenty-one technologies were available; a complete list appears in Appendix B.

ATW III

In ATW III, also a baseline effort, the teams used the casualties gen-erated in ATWs I and II and reorganized and reallocated the more robust HSS provided for ATW I to determine whether it could better deal with the casualty care challenges. Otherwise, the scenario, length of battle, and other characteristics replicated those of ATWs I and II.

ATW IV

This workshop mirrored the first three in its general structure, but it expanded the scope in terms of echelon and length of battle. Based in part on the initial workshops, the AMEDD determined that a 44-bed CSH would likely be insufficient, and it set out to determine what HSS system would be required at echelons above UA. ATW IV as-sessed the medical risk and demand that 76 casualties from a single UA would create for an echelons-above-UA HSS system during a simulated 12-hour battle. Two teams of subject matter experts re-viewed the casualty results of a combat simulation and determined the disposition of the casualties. Team members had the same range of skills that the members of the first three workshops did. The

AMEDD C&S provided the UA HSS structure, and the team members decided how to employ it. The HSS structure was based on the future organizational and operational concepts being considered by the AMEDD and the Army at the time of the workshops. It included a medic with each platoon, evacuation vehicles with each company, evacuation and treatment vehicles at the battalion, and a medical company with an attached FST and forward support medevac team at the brigade.

Although this workshop paralleled the first three in its general structure, it differed in its purpose and the specifics of execution. It was designed primarily to begin the analysis to estimate the medical demand on the echelons above the UA.

Conducted in February 2004, ATW IV used the Caspian 2.0 scenario and results from the JANUS simulation to determine Blue losses. The scenario involved an augmented Future Combat Systems (FCS)-equipped UA brigade fighting several enemy brigades over 12 hours. The most important Blue mission was to help reinstate a friendly government requesting assistance. This mission focused on isolating the strategic center of gravity (capital region). The Blue side also had to defeat antigovernment enemy forces in the country. Blue was further tasked to deter any third-country intervention on the side of the rebel forces. It also had to cut the lines of communication from the capital region toward the south to this regional power.

The battlefield was 75 x 85 kilometers. The terrain was characterized by foothills and rugged mountainous terrain, urban and other complex terrain, a large reservoir, rivers, and an irrigation complex in a large, extensive valley flood plain consisting of canals and ditches. Enemy forces included three corps, organized around 12 maneuver brigades. There were over 40,000 troops, 2,000 armored fighting vehicles, 450 air defense systems, and 600 artillery systems simulated. Red also employed about 3,800 man-portable air defense systems across its forces. Most of Red's forces remained concealed in well-prepared defensive positions in the urban areas in an attempt to preserve combat power and to draw Blue forces into these spaces for an urban fight.

The simulation for this workshop was JANUS, an interactive ground combat simulation featuring high-resolution graphics. The model is stochastic, that is, it assesses battlefield phenomena, the result of one combat vehicle firing at another, according to the laws of probability and chance. JANUS is designed primarily to allow a user to model military conflicts of opposing forces up to the brigade level. The forces are simultaneously directed and controlled by a set of players or gamers for each side who have knowledge only of enemy units that one or more of their subordinate units can observe directly. Additional intelligence from other sources may be available if the appropriate command, control, and communication nets are represented. JANUS is played on a computer-generated, digitized terrain map that is displayed via color graphics monitors; it includes representations of terrain features such as elevation (i.e., contour lines), roads, rivers, vegetation, buildings, and so forth. The simulation determines both Blue and Red force losses.

As with the earlier workshops, individual casualties were tracked. In this case, however, they were not tracked outside the UA. They were treated within the UA and either returned to duty or became a demand on the HSS system at echelons above the UA.

ATW V

This workshop also followed the general structure of the previous ones, with subject matter experts reviewing the casualty results of a combat simulation. The principal focus of ATW V was to continue the process of establishing the casualty demand data that must be addressed by the echelons-above-UA HSS system. It involved four UAs (and supporting Units of Employment [UEs]), with 429 casualties over a 100-hour simulated battle. Thus, the principal purpose of ATW V was to provide analytical support to the AMEDD to assist it in designing the HSS system above the UA level. It, too, employed teams of subject matter experts.[3] Again, the scope expanded. This battle involved four UAs and soldiers from the UEs, the echelons above the UA. It featured an attack to isolate a city as part of an effort to restore a legitimate government, and combat lasted for over 100 hours. It used the Vector-in-Command (VIC) simulation rather than the JANUS simulation used for ATW IV. The battlefield expanded considerably over previous workshops, reaching 500 x 225 kilometers. The medical structure provided to each brigade-sized UA mirrored that provided the UA in ATW IV.

---

[3] Although the workshop used two teams of subject matter experts, the 429 casualties were divided between them. Thus, only one team evaluated each casualty, which is why Table 2.1 reflects only one subject matter expert evaluation for each casualty.

CHAPTER THREE

Workshop Results

Each workshop focused on a series of questions and issues. The questions were posed to the teams at the outset of the workshop, and the teams were asked to provide their answers at the end, basing them empirically on the workshop outcomes. The issues were addressed within *"The Day After . . ."* methodology that RAND developed to deal with questions of nuclear proliferation policy (Millot, Molander, and Wilson, 1993). This methodology requires players to assess the issues in light of the workshop outcomes. For the ATWs, the teams were asked to use what they learned about the response of the HSS system during the workshops to formulate their suggestions. Table 3.1 shows the questions posed to and issues addressed by each workshop in the order that they actually occurred at the workshops. The results of the workshops and the responses of the teams follow the order of the table. Not all workshops dealt with all questions and issues.

Questions

What was the final disposition of the casualties at the end of the workshop?

Table 3.2 shows the casualty rates across the five workshops as a percentage of the population at risk. By and large, these casualty rates roughly parallel historical ones. Comparing casualties across conflicts

Table 3.1
Questions and Issues Addressed by the ATWs

Questions/Issues	ATW I	ATW II	ATW III	ATW IV	ATW V
Questions					
What was the final disposition of the casualties at the end of the workshop?	√	√	√	√	√
What was the status of the HSS system (i.e., the availability of medical resources and services) at the end of the workshop?	√	√	√	√ ·	√
What advice would the teams give on the ability of the HSS system to support continued operations?	√	√	√		
How many casualties require further evacuation and treatment at echelons above the UA?				√	√
Issues					
Where do first responders and combat medics fit in the overall future concept for combat casualty care, and what treatment capabilities (technologies and skills) will medics require to support this concept?	√	√	√	√	√
What theater military medical infrastructure is necessary to support future military medical operations across the spectrum of operations?	√	√	√	√	√
What are the evacuation requirements to support military operations across the spectrum of operations?	√	√	√	√	√
What are AMEDD's platform (ground and aerial evacuation and treatment system) requirements to support the transformed force and on which of these platforms would telemedicine (and other technologies, e.g., en route care) be advantageous?	√	√	√	√	√
What technologies would significantly improve force health protection (how much are they worth at the margin)?	√	√	√	√	√

involves as much art as it does science because the intensity of the combat varies within and across conflicts and because the meaning of terms has changed over time. Further, changes in operational medicine concepts—such as advances in surgical care, placing that care farther forward on the battlefield, and advances in evacuation capabilities—have changed the distribution among casualty outcomes.

Table 3.2
Workshop Casualty Rates

Workshop	Casualties (KIA + WIA)	Population at Risk	Percentage	Daily Average	Daily Percentage
ATWs I–III	54	1,039	5.2	162	15
ATW IV	76	2,499	3.0	152	6
ATW V	429	14,000	3.0	102	1

Inevitably, only gross comparisons are possible. Using casualties as a percentage of the force involved shows that the 5 percent casualty rate experienced in ATWs I and II (54/1,039) falls within historical ranges. Even extrapolating casualties over a full day of battle does not yield unusually high rates. As R. F. Bellamy explains:

> Battle casualty rates are inversely proportional to the size of the unit; for example, a battalion will have a higher rate than a division. There is an obvious explanation for this fact: the smaller the combat unit, the fewer the combat support and combat service support personnel, who . . . are not exposed to direct enemy fire. When combat units are actually in contact with the enemy, division battle casualty rates in high-intensity war have usually been about 1% per day, although on rare occasions rates of up to 10% per day have been observed. Corresponding brigade and battalion rates are 3% and 10% per day, respectively (Bellamy, 1995, p. 6).

ATWs I and II resulted in two overall casualty outcomes, which averaged the results of the three teams for each workshop. Although the HSS structure differed in each, the results were remarkably similar, as the averages reported in Table 3.3 show.

The similarity of the results suggests that the different HSS resources between ATW I and II were not the limiting factor. Recall that each maneuver platoon in ATW I had a medic, and those in ATW II did not. Evacuation vehicles were also cut back. Yet the reduction made little difference in outcomes.

Table 3.3
Average Casualties by Outcome in ATWs I and II at H+8

Outcome	ATW I		ATW II	
	Number	Percentage	Number	Percentage
Killed in action	15.7	29	17.0	31
Died of wounds	2.0	4	3.0	6
Returned to duty	3.7	7	3.3	6
Treated/held or awaiting treatment[a]	32.7	61	30.7	57

NOTES: H+8 equals 8 hours after H hour, which is when combat operations begin. Means are calculated from the results of three teams per workshop. Although 57 casualties occurred, three were U.S. Air Force pilots and were not counted here; thus N = 54. ATW III is not listed because it used the casualties generated by ATW II to support its analysis of the reconfigured HSS system.

[a]Some casualties were held after treatment, e.g., awaiting evacuation.

Note that the results shown in Table 3.3 do not indicate the final disposition of the casualties awaiting treatment or being held after treatment, e.g., awaiting evacuation, at H+8 (8 hours after H hour, which is when combat operations begin). After H+8, the number of soldiers who die of their wounds will either hold constant or increase, and most workshop participants thought they would increase.

The combat posited by the scenario in ATW IV involved more intense fighting, and it ran longer than in the first three workshops—12 hours compared with 8. The UA sustained 76 casualties. Their breakout appears in Table 3.4.

Table 3.4
Average Casualties by Outcome in ATW IV at H+12

Outcome	Number	Percentage
Killed in action	6	8
Died of wounds	4	5
Returned to duty	11	14
Evacuated to UE or awaiting evacuation in the UA[a]	56	74

NOTE: Numbers do not total 76 because of rounding.
[a]Includes 15 patients in surgery at FST who will require evacuation to UE.

We cannot determine the final disposition of all casualties because the capabilities of the echelons-above-UA HSS system remain to be determined. ATW IV assumed that casualties requiring evacuation outside the UA were evacuated as soon as that determination was made. This assumption supported the goal of determining the demand on echelons above the UA and simultaneously freed up UA medical assets. Had this assumption not been made, the casualties would have overwhelmed UA capabilities, and it would not have been possible to determine the demand on the higher echelons. Table 3.4 lists only the casualties for whom a definitive outcome was possible.[1] What ultimately happens to them will be determined by the capabilities at the UE.

The teams considered two other strategies in addition to rapid evacuation. One called for treating the casualty as close to the site of the injury as possible (called persistence-in-combat). Taken to the extreme, this strategy relies on advanced technologies, some self-applied by the individual soldier and some automatically applied. A second strategy delays the evacuation until the battle is over and then evacuates all casualties. The persistence-in-combat strategy has outcomes similar to that of rapid evacuation. This may mean that the demand on the HSS system was so high that a de facto persistence strategy resulted. The subject matter experts concluded that delayed evacuation would result in significantly higher morbidity and mortality.

The ATW V scenario resulted in 429 casualties during the approximately 100 hours of combat. The casualties and types appear in Table 3.5. The rates of casualties who were killed in action and who died of their wounds were similar to those of the other workshops. A

---

[1] Once the medical personnel in the UA delivered the care they could at that level and a casualty could not return to duty (i.e., he was injured beyond a return-to-duty level), he was marked as ready for immediate evacuation to the UE level. The ultimate disposition of these casualties was unknown. We note as well that 15 patients who had been treated at the UA—listed as "in surgery at the FST"—were determined to need further care. They also would be evacuated to the UE. Thus, in total, 51 patients (about two-thirds of all casualties), needed to be evacuated to the UE level.

Table 3.5
Average Casualties by Type in ATW V at
H+72

Outcome	Number	Percentage
Killed in action	35	8
Died of wounds	16	4
Returned to duty	110	26
Evacuated or awaiting evacuation in the UA	268	62

significant difference was the number of casualties who lost limbs. One-fifth of the surviving casualties who were wounded seriously enough to be removed from combat either lost a limb or would likely do so if they lived long enough to be treated at echelons above the UA. A portion of these limb losses was likely unpreventable, based on the description of the wounds. However, 22 casualties were described as having salvageable limb wounds, but the limbs were amputated nonetheless, representing 38 percent of the total estimated amputations. One likely reason for these rates of limb loss was surgical capacity: Casualties who were delayed in the surgical queue in order to save another's life through surgery may have lost a limb as a result. Another plausible explanation is the delay in time from wounding to surgery; casualties with vascular extremity injuries often require prompt surgery to save the limb.

What was the status of the HSS system (i.e., the availability of medical resources and services) at the end of the workshop?
Generally, the medical system was at or near capacity, especially surgical capabilities. In ATWs I–III, the HSS system was at capacity by hour 8, and the subject matter experts estimated it would take several hours to clear the surgical backlogs at the FST and the CSH. Ground evacuation assets were not fully used, but air evacuation capabilities were at or near capacity. Furthermore, medical supplies and blood were either exhausted or in short supply. ATW IV assumed that casualties were evacuated out of the UA almost as soon as the need to do so was recognized. It was not possible to determine the backlog at the

UA, because it depends on the capabilities above the UA, which remain unknown. That said, it is possible to assess the use of the UA HSS system based on plans and doctrine. For example, teams were able to assess surgical requirements for the FST based on the nature of the casualties. As the battle progressed, surgical need climbed. Based on one team's analysis, demand for operating tables exceeded supply after about three hours of combat. Demand also outstripped supply of recovery cots, but not until about hour 7 of fighting. Evacuation assets were also taxed at or near their maximum capacity.

Examination of the overall performance of the HSS system is instructive. One way to gauge its performance is to determine how long it takes a casualty to receive surgery after being wounded. The metric used here was to determine if a casualty arrived at a medical treatment facility within an hour.[2] In ATW IV, the delay exceeded one hour in every case, with times ranging from 69 to 413 minutes. In ATW V, as was the case for earlier workshops, HSS systems operated at full capacity for most of the scenario. Surgical capabilities were most taxed: UA FSTs performed 118 surgeries that took about 114 hours, not counting pre- and post-operative procedures. This level of activity represents about six surgeries per 24 hours for each of the four FSTs. Recall that an FST is structured to perform 10 surgeries in 24 hours, but only for 72 hours. However, demand did not spread evenly among the UAs or over time. The number of surgical cases per FST

---

[2] Some refer to this period as the "golden hour." The golden hour concept was first advanced by D. D. Trunkey (1983), who showed that about half of the civilian deaths that resulted from blunt trauma occurred within the first hour. Others, such as Bellamy (1995, pp. 15–16), have argued that these data do not translate well to military circumstances, where penetration rather than blunt trauma causes the bulk of the casualties and most casualties of penetrating trauma die within 10 minutes. However, Bellamy also points out that, "the longer a casualty remains on the battlefield, he is not only more likely to die from his original wound, but he is also more likely to receive a new and possibly more-lethal wound," (1995, p. 14). Thus, evacuation time is not irrelevant. Most casualties in Vietnam were evacuated to a treatment facility within an hour (Bellamy, 1995, p. 14), and thus, one hour is a reasonable metric to gauge the efficiency of the evacuation system.

ranged from 18 in UA2 to 46 in UA4.[3] Figure 3.1 shows the number of surgeries performed and the time that each FST was operating at surgical capacity, i.e., performing surgery on two patients.

The subject matter experts carefully managed the triage of the patients, often delaying surgery on one patient so that a more seriously wounded individual could receive it. As mentioned above, this practice may have contributed to the increased number of amputations. Evacuation assets were used to near capacity. It is difficult to tease apart delays caused by evacuation from those caused by surgical backlog, but the mean delay time from injury to surgery for those requiring surgery at the FST was 7.5 hours, with a range from 1 to nearly 21 hours. Virtually none of them were treated within an hour.

Figure 3.1
Time Periods When FSTs Were at Maximum Capacity

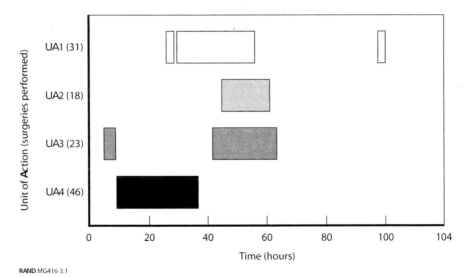

RAND MG416-3.1

---

[3] Distributing surgical cases among FSTs (providing lateral support between UAs) was not possible because of the distances involved and because FSTs were moving to keep up with their respective UAs.

These times were longer than those for ATW IV (mean delay of 2.7 hours). Possible explanations for this difference are the early peaks in casualty flow, more casualties overall, and high demand on the FSTs during the ATW V scenario, resulting in surgical backlogs.

What advice would the teams give on the ability of the HSS system to support continued operations?

Each team in the first three workshops judged that the casualties had saturated the HSS system, and they agreed that they would recommend an operational pause to the maneuver commander so that the HSS could treat the existing casualties and restore its capabilities. We note that this recommendation is at odds with the current Army doctrine of sustained, continuous operations.

How many casualties require further evacuation and treatment at echelons above the UA?

A primary goal of ATW IV was to determine the demand on the HSS system at echelons above the UA. Both teams estimated similar demands for evacuation to and treatment by the UE. These estimates appear in Figure 3.2. *Urgent* and *priority* are categories that determine the priority of care and evacuation. An urgent designation is assigned to casualties who should be evacuated as soon as possible with a maximum delay of two hours. Priority is the designation assigned to sick and wounded who should be evacuated within four hours or their condition will degrade to the point that they will fall into the urgent category (U.S. Department of the Army, 2000a, p. 7-2).

Similar to the results in ATW IV, about two-thirds of the ATW V casualties required evacuation to higher echelons. As Figure 3.3 shows, about 80 percent (213 of 268) of those evacuated were classified as urgent or priority.

Figure 3.2
Number of Casualties Evacuated to UE in ATW IV

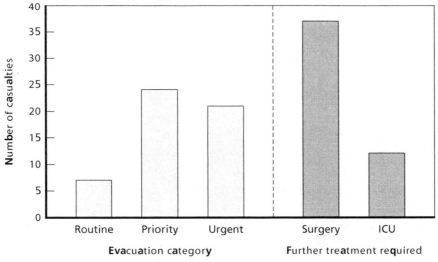

Evacuation category   Further treatment required

Figure 3.3
Number of Casualties Evacuated to UE in ATW V

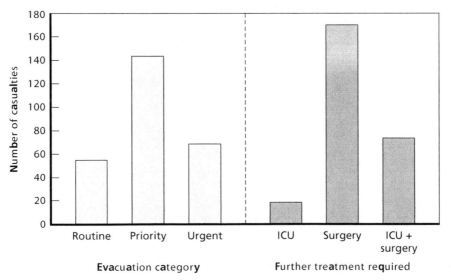

Evacuation category   Further treatment required

Issues

Each team was asked to address the issues retrospectively. They did so by means of a guided discussion, focusing on the issues in the context of the scenario, the critical factors that contributed to the outcomes, and the implications for the AMEDD and the Army if these factors were not present.

Where do first responders and combat medics fit in the overall future concept for combat casualty care, and what treatment capabilities (technologies and skills) will medics require to support this concept?

All ATW teams judged the assumed proficiency of the first responders—particularly the combat lifesavers—and the availability of advanced technologies to control bleeding as essential. The lack of combat medics in the maneuver platoons in ATW II made this capability even more critical. The nature of the scenarios—individual combat vehicles operating far apart from each other—means that when a vehicle is hit by enemy fire, other crew members must provide the immediate medical care unless a combat medic happens to be riding in the vehicle. One team estimated that 46 percent of the combat deaths could have been precluded had a combat medic been closer to the casualty, assuming rapid subsequent evacuation.

Some participants doubted that the level of combat lifesaver proficiency assumed in the scenario could be achieved or sustained if achieved. A related observation was that the role of the combat lifesaver was unreasonably large in light of the pace of the battle, and the expectation of medical proficiency was high. In the view of the subject matter experts, the skills assumed by the workshops in reality approach what is expected of a 91W combat medic. To earn the 91W Military Occupational Specialty requires 16 weeks of training.

The role and importance of the combat lifesaver raises several issues that need further analysis. First, there was broad consensus that the training and sustaining of the skills assumed of a combat lifesaver need to be thoroughly assessed to determine feasibility, considering the proficiency levels demanded by the workshops. In short, is it possible to train a future soldier to be both an infantryman and a highly competent combat lifesaver and to maintain both skill sets over time? Second, performing as a combat lifesaver will be a secondary role for UA combat arms soldiers, just as it is now. Consequently, individuals designated as combat lifesavers will face an inherent tension during combat between providing combat casualty care and fighting. In these workshops, the combat lifesaver was assumed to provide care and thus contributed significantly to favorable casualty outcomes. However, the workshops did not assess the effect of these soldiers being diverted from their combat duties.

Any alternatives suggested that did not include force structure changes required an even higher level of combat lifesaver competence and the ability to provide substantial treatment during evacuation. The reliance on the combat lifesaver and the advanced medical technologies was intended to deal with the problems caused by dispersed operations and the lack of organic medics in the maneuver platoon. The combination of these two challenges means that substantial time passes between injury and care by a medic. Bleeding was seen as the most significant battle injury; thus the advanced technologies were critical as was the need to apply them as soon as possible. The technologies included hemostatic agents, fibrin bandages, advanced tourniquets, and advanced intravenous fluids. One ATW I team judged that had not the combat lifesavers been as proficient in applying these technologies as they were, the mortality rate (KIA + DOW) would have risen from the 33 percent it assessed to 59 percent.

The issue of the combat medic goes hand in glove with that of the combat lifesaver. The workshop subject matter experts concluded that the highly dispersed, fast-moving operations called into question the role of the platoon combat medic. The principal issue was the proximity of the platoon medic to casualties. If the casualty was not in the same vehicle as the medic, the distance to the casualty was generally at least a kilometer. Consequently, it was not feasible for the medic to move by foot to the casualty. This created a dilemma that was recognized, but not solved, by workshop participants. To move the medic to the casualty, the FCS vehicle carrying the medic would have to be diverted from the mission. Such a decision would degrade platoon combat capability. In the workshop, this dilemma was largely solved, as noted above, by giving the combat lifesaver extraordinary medical competence and capabilities, principally in the form of advanced medical technologies. The best assistance the medic could potentially provide in these cases was remote advice.

This does not imply that Future Force medics will not play an important role in other dimensions of force health protection. As is the case today, they will be involved in training combat lifesavers and other soldiers, performing on-site and remote triage during battle, dealing with disease and non-battle injuries, and myriad other readiness-related duties that have traditionally fallen to combat medics. What the workshops did highlight, however, was the immense difficulty that combat medics will have in providing immediate response to casualties in dispersed, fast-moving combat operations.

The teams in ATW III concluded that the battlefield roles of the combat lifesaver, the maneuver platoon medic, and the battalion aid station need to be revisited. That is, they questioned whether the platoon medic and the battalion aid station could continue to fulfill their traditional roles effectively and whether the skills assumed for the combat lifesaver were appropriate or even feasible.

What theater military medical infrastructure is necessary to support future military medical operations across the spectrum of operations?

All teams regarded the HSS structure (14 ground treatment/evacuation vehicles, three air ambulances, a CSH, and a medical company with an FST supporting a battalion) in ATW I as generous. As rich as the structure was, all teams thought the casualties sustained over eight hours would tax it. Even though the structure in ATW II was reduced from that in ATW I, it still represented a large dedication of divisional assets to support one battalion. This HSS structure was also taxed. The ATW III team saw dispersion of units, long lines of communication, and limited surgical capability as the most problematic aspects of the scenario. All affected timely surgical intervention, which was seen as imperative to preserve lives. But, because of the demand, the team drew little distinction between the FST and the CSH, which represents a change in the doctrinal position that the FST stabilizes a relatively small (about 15 percent) proportion of patients for further evacuation. Because of the relatively high demand and because the geographical difference disappeared as the battle progressed, casualties were evacuated to whichever facility had available capacity. Modular alternatives to provide more surgical capacity forward may prove attractive, but mobility and security raise significant concerns in this scenario. All ATW teams indicated that the perfect situational awareness provided by the WPSM was a key capability because it enabled an optimal allocation of medical assets.

ATWs I–III required all surgeries to be done at the FST or CSH. In ATW V, surgeries could be performed at the UA or the patient could be stabilized and evacuated to higher echelons. However, in ATW V, casualties also backed up at the FST, and the subject matter experts carefully managed the surgical queue, judging that some casualties would not survive further evacuation without stabilizing surgery. The residual load of UA casualties requiring surgery will place a heavy demand for surgical capability in echelons above the UA. Also, as was the case in the earlier workshops, the FST could not displace forward as the battle progressed because it was performing surgeries. Thus, the distance between the point of injury and the operating table gradually increased.

Additionally, some evidence suggests that the demand for surgery and postsurgical care could increase in the future, particularly given recent experiences in Iraq (Bowen, 2003; Patel et al., 2004). Emerging casualty data from Iraq are demonstrating the effect that improved soldier protection and advanced medical technologies are having on casualty outcomes. Better body armor and medical technologies have combined to enable soldiers who would have been killed in earlier conflicts to survive to reach an operating table, where their lives are frequently saved. In Iraq, the number of casualties over time has not created an excessive demand on the HSS system. Nevertheless, a reduction in KIA and DOW rates could drive up demand on surgical capacity and postsurgical care in the types of operations depicted in the scenario used in ATW V—a demand that the envisioned UA HSS system has had difficulty dealing with in ATWs I–IV.

Figure 3.4 illustrates the nature of the evacuation problem in ATW V. The diamond shapes mark where the casualties occurred (this diagram was drawn from another source where the colors of the diamond shapes were significant. They are not in this context). Each part of the grid overlaid on the map is 50 kilometers on a side or 250 square kilometers. A Blackhawk medevac helicopter can cruise at about 140 knots per hour (about 260 kilometers per hour) and can fly for just over two hours without refueling (U.S. Department of the Army, 2000b). Thus, the round trip to evacuate a casualty on this battlefield could easily be more than 600 kilometers, which could take more than two hours at nominal cruising speed and comes close to the helicopter's un-refueled range. Such evacuation distances would allow very little time on the ground.

Figure 3.4
Battlefield Distances in ATW V

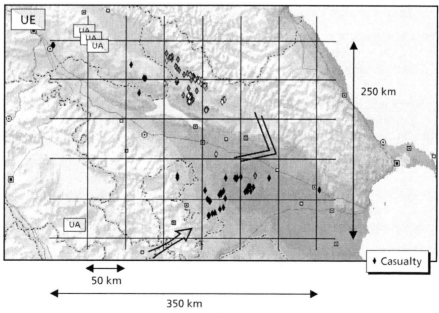

RAND MG416-3.4

What are the evacuation requirements to support military operations across the spectrum of operations?

The dispersion of the units made air evacuation critical. Each team in ATWs I–III fully employed the three Blackhawk medical evacuation helicopters and thought that they would be needed for some time after H+8 to evacuate the casualties that occurred in the first eight hours. The throughput of the casualties stressed the HSS system used in the simulation. Although all the teams recommended pushing additional surgical capabilities forward, by doctrine the FST is intended to stabilize patients for evacuation. As one medical expert put it, "[FST] surgical strategy aims for damage control, not definitive repair" (Gawande, 2004, p. 2473). Placing additional assets that could evacuate patients out of theater further forward might reduce the criticality of surgical capability in the rear of the theater.

What are AMEDD's platform (ground and aerial evacuation and treatment system) requirements to support the transformed force and on which of these platforms would telemedicine (and other technologies, e.g., en route care) be advantageous?

In all scenarios, the Blackhawk medevac helicopters were critical in clearing the battlefield, often spelling the difference between life and death. They became increasingly important as the distance between the point of injury and the UA medical assets increased over the engagement. As evacuation distances increase, as they did in the later workshops, air evacuation becomes increasingly problematic, especially when the evacuation distance exceeds the medevac helicopter's flight range.

What technologies would significantly improve force health protection (how much are they worth at the margin)?

Table 3.1 indicates that all workshops considered advanced medical technologies, but the teams did not directly assess the effects of the medical technologies on medical outcomes. Although the performance of medical technologies was not a stated issue in the workshops, participants noted several technologies that they believed were critical to combat casualty care during the workshops. As has been noted, the most challenging aspects of the scenarios from a medical treatment perspective were the dispersion of the forces across the battlefield and the distance from the injury site to the FST. Perhaps the most important technology in the workshops for dealing with the dispersion factor was the WPSM, which provided immediate location and injury-type data for all casualties. This information was invaluable in the medical regulation effort, particularly in allocating evacuation assets. The distance factor for urgent casualties was primarily alleviated by the application of a number of advanced hemostatic agents (often applied by a combat lifesaver), which prevented fatal hemorrhage while severely wounded casualties were en route to treatment at the FST. Absent these two critical technologies, casualty outcomes would have been worse.

CHAPTER FOUR

Conclusions and Implications

Although the primary purpose of the five ATWs was to answer the questions posed at the outset of each workshop and address the issues raised, our analysis of the results of the workshops led us to broader conclusions and suggested some wider implications for the HSS system and for the Army at large. Here we present those conclusions and implications.

Conclusions

We drew three conclusions from the workshops. The first is that the medical capabilities of the UA and the dispersion of forces pose significant challenges for the HSS system. The movement of a wounded soldier from the point of injury to the place of treatment is, to state the obvious, a function of time and distance. The dispersion envisioned for the Future Force has important implications. One is that it is unlikely that a combat medic will be nearby when an injury occurs. Thus, the importance of trained combat lifesavers increases, because they are very likely to be the immediate and possibly only source of medical care until the casualty arrives at the FST (unless the patient gets medical attention on the evacuation vehicle).

Second, both ATWs IV and V indicated that the HSS system at echelons above the UA would receive significant demands to treat and evacuate patients. Because the HSS structure at those echelons remains to be defined, the workshops could not determine the disposition of the patients treated at those echelons, but it was clear that it would be a substantial number.

Finally, additional Future Force simulations and scenarios are needed, and the AMEDD needs to continue to test its HSS system concepts against the results. As we noted earlier, the games used only a few scenarios and simulations, which limits the insights and conclusions drawn from the workshops. Much remains to be resolved, particularly with respect to medical support at echelons above the UA, and simulations will assist in this regard. Simulations and scenarios should also expand to explore the issues associated with rear area operations, which could pose a special challenge for AMEDD units.

Implications

Analysis of the workshop results identified two important implications that transcend those the AMEDD can address. They merit attention at the Army level.

Lines of Communication and Rear Area Security

As the battle portrayed in this scenario progressed, the lines of communication steadily lengthened and were left largely unsecured as maneuver units pressed on to their objectives. From the perspective of the HSS system, this situation required ground medical evacuation vehicles to move independently to casualty locations, casualty collection points, aerial medical evacuation landing zones, and so forth, across a battlefield that was neither cleared nor secured. This situation is not dissimilar to the challenges faced by coalition forces during Operation Iraqi Freedom in securing lines of communication behind combat forces rapidly moving toward Baghdad. Additionally, as already noted, the FST had to stay in place to perform its mission. A reasonable assumption is that the FST and the UA medical company would require some level of defense during this time, as would other support units. As noted earlier, the workshops assumed no attrition of any of the components of the HSS system in order to portray its capabilities in a best-case condition given the scenarios used. Therefore,

the effect of operating in an insecure rear area was not specifically assessed. Nevertheless, it is reasonable to assume that elements of the
HSS system would be attacked, particularly if they moved around the
battlefield as single entities. Loss of medical personnel or platforms
could only worsen medical outcomes. The issue for the Army is how
ground and air lines of communication and rear areas will be secured
in the wake of rapidly advancing Future Force combat units.

Unit Morale, Cohesion, and Combat Effectiveness on a Dispersed Battlefield

The shaping operation examined in ATWs I–III took place on a dispersed battlefield across which UA forces rapidly advanced to their
objectives. As combat units advanced rapidly, disabled vehicles and
their crews were left behind. Again, the growing rear area in which
these vehicles and crews found themselves was not secure, and one
could assume the crews were still vulnerable to attack from either
paramilitary forces or isolated elements of regular forces. Team members believed that the nature of the scenario's battlefield—dispersed
forces and not secure—would create problems in the realms of morale, cohesion, and combat effectiveness in a number of ways. First, as
already discussed, getting a combat medic to a casualty location was
frequently not feasible, and casualties often only received initial care
from a combat lifesaver. This situation contrasts with the historical
expectation of American soldiers and their leaders: When they call for
a medic, one appears. Second, given the dispersion of the battlefield
and the distance among casualties, medical evacuation platforms, and
treatment locations, the elapsed time between wounding and evacuation was generally longer than the Army has come to expect. Team
members believed that the frustration of the twin expectations that a
medic will quickly aid a casualty and that the wounded person will if
necessary be rapidly evacuated to the appropriate level of care could
negatively affect morale, cohesion, and combat effectiveness. Furthermore, the possibility of being "abandoned" on a battlefield that
has not been secured would only complicate these issues. These areas
of Future Force operations need investigation.

Subject Matter Experts

Table A.1
ATW I Subject Matter Experts

Subject Matter Area	Team 1	Team 2	Team 3
Aerial evacuation	COL David Heintz	LTC William Layden	LTC Bryan Harp
AMEDD doctrine	LTC Richard Dabbs	LTC Bernard Hebron	LTC Brian Shaw
Medical operations/ground evacuation	MAJ Chris Richards	MAJ Bruce Shabaz	MAJ Thomas Berry
Anesthesiology	COL John Chiles	COL Denver Perkins	COL Stephen Janny
Combat medic	SGM Eduardo Benavides	SFC Michael Haynes	SFC Louis Gholston
Medical technology	COL Robert Vandre	LTC Beau Freund	Dr. Tommy Morris
Orthopedics	LTC Paul Dougherty	COL John Uhorchak	COL James Malcolm
Physician assistant	MAJ Jerald Wells	CPT Peter Bulley	MAJ Michael Summers
General surgery	LTC Brian Lein	LTC Stephen Flarherty	LTC Kim Marley
Trauma	COL David Burris		LTC Tom Knuth

Table A.2
ATW II Subject Matter Experts

Subject Matter Area	Team 1	Team 2	Team 3
Aerial evacuation	COL David Heintz	LTC William Layden	LTC Bryan Harp
AMEDD doctrine	LTC Richard Dabbs	LTC Bernard Hebron	LTC Brian Shaw
Medical operations/ground evacuation	MAJ Chris Richards	MAJ Bruce Shabaz	MAJ Keith Rigdon
Anesthesiology	COL John Chiles	COL Denver Perkins	COL Stephen Janny
Combat medic	SGM Eduardo Benavides	SFC Michael Haynes	SFC Louis Gholston
Medical technology	COL Robert Vandre	LTC Beau Freund	Dr. Tommy Morris
Orthopedics	LTC Paul Dougherty	COL John Uhorchak	MAJ Bradley Nelson
Physician assistant	MAJ Jerald Wells	CPT Peter Bulley	MAJ Michael Summers
General surgery	LTC Brian Lein	LTC Stephen Flarherty	LTC Kim Marley
Trauma	COL David Burris		LTC Tom Knuth/ LTC Jim Goth
Unit of Action	Mr. Rick Pena		
Combat Service Support		Ms. Gladys Garcia/LTC Mel Washington	

Table A.3
ATW III Subject Matter Experts

Subject Matter Area	Team 1	Team 2	Team 3
Aerial evacuation	COL David Heintz	LTC William Layden	
AMEDD doctrine	LTC Richard Dabbs	LTC Bernard Hebron	LTC Brian Shaw
Medical operations/ground evacuation	MAJ Chris Richards	MAJ Bruce Shabaz	MAJ Bob Cornes
Anesthesiology	COL John Chiles	COL Denver Perkins	COL Stephen Janny
Combat medic	SGM Eduardo Benavides	SFC Michael Haynes	SFC Louis Gholston
Medical technology	COL Robert Vandre	LTC Beau Freund	Dr. Tommy Morris
Orthopedics		COL John Uhorchak	MAJ Bradley Nelson
Physician assistant	MAJ Jerald Wells	CPT Peter Bulley	MAJ Michael Summers
General surgery	LTC Brian Lein	LTC Stephen Flarherty	LTC Kim Marley
Trauma	COL David Burris		LTC Tom Knuth
Unit of Action	Mr. Rick Pena		LTC Mel Washington
Combat Service Support		Ms. Gladys Garcia	

Table A.4
ATW IV Subject Matter Experts

Subject Matter Area	Team 1	Team 2
Team leader/surgery	COL Thomas Knuth	COL Kim Marley
Surgery	MAJ Richard Pope	COL David Burris
Nursing	LTC Kathleen Ryan	COL Anita Schmidt
Physician's assistant	CPT Dawn Orta	1LT Michael Smith
Combat medic (91W)	MSG Steven Kerrick	SSG Scott Adkins
Combat stress	COL James Stokes	LTC Willis Leavitt
Evacuation	LTC William Layden	LTC Tim Moore
Logistics	CPT Jennifer Humphries	Mr. Gerry LoSardo
Medical technology	Mr. David Smart	MAJ Robert Wildzunas
Unit of Action	Mr. Dave Hardin	Mr. Jim Brazaele
Medical company	CPT James Morrison	CPT Jon Baker
Command, control, communications, computers, and intelligence	CPT Kevin Peck	LTC DaCosta Barrow

Table A.5
ATW V Subject Matter Experts

Subject Matter Area	Team 1	Team 2
Team leader/surgery	COL Thomas Knuth	MAJ Richard Pope
Surgery		Dr. Huang
Nursing	LTC Kathleen Ryan	COL Anita Schmidt
Physician's Asst.	CPT Dawn Orta	1LT Michael Smith
Combat medic (91W)	MSG Steven Kerrick	SSG Scott Adkins
Evacuation	MAJ Fristoe	LTC Tim Moore
Medical technology	Mr. David Smart	
Unit of Action	Mr. Dave Hardin	Mr. Jim Brazaele
Medical company	CPT James Morrison	CPT Jon Baker

Medical Technologies Employed in ATWs

The following advanced medical technologies, deemed by Medical Research and Materiel Command (MRMC) to be feasible and due to be fielded by 2015, were employed by the workshop participants. These technologies and their descriptions were developed for use during ATWs I–IV. MRMC asked that the same technologies be used for ATW V. A more extensive discussion of these technologies appears in Johnson and Cecchine (2004, Appendix C).

1. Warfighter Physiological Status Monitor (WPSM)
2. Universal Red Blood Cells for Severe Hemorrhage
3. Universal Freeze-Dried Plasma
4. Spray-on Protective Bandage
5. Machine Language Translation
6. Liquid Tourniquet
7. Lightweight Extremity Splint
8. Intravenous (IV) Hemostatic Drug
9. Intracavitary Hemostatic Agent
10. Enzymatic Wound Debridement
11. Battlefield Medical Information System
12. Advanced Resuscitation Fluid
13. Advanced Hemostatic Dressing
14. Warrior Medic (biocorder)
15. Hemoglobin-Based Oxygen Carrier
16. Field Therapy for Laser Eye Injury
17. Digital Information and Communication System

18. Transportable Automated Life Support System
19. Teleconsultation/Teledermatology
20. High-Intensity Focused Ultrasound
21. Forward-Deployable Digital Medical Treatment Facility

Bibliography

Anderson, Robert H., and Anthony C. Hearn, *An Exploration of Cyberspace Security R&D Investment Strategies for DARPA: "The Day After—in Cyberspace II,"* Santa Monica, Calif.: RAND Corporation, MR-797-DARPA, 1996.

Bellamy, Ronald F., "Anesthesia and Perioperative Care of the Combat Casualty (Part IV: Surgical Combat Casualty Care)," in Russ Zajtchuk and Christopher M. Grande, eds., *Textbook of Military Medicine*, Washington, D.C.: Office of the Surgeon General, 1995.

Bowen, David, "U.S. Troops Injuries Showed Body Armor's Value," *Washington Post*, May 4, 2003, p. A 20.

Dolev, E., "Medical Service in the Lebanon War, 1982: An Overview," *Israeli Journal of Medical Science*, Vol. 20, April 1984, pp. 297–299.

Gawande, Atul, "Casualties of War—Military Care for the Wounded from Iraq and Afghanistan," *New England Journal of Medicine*, Vol. 351, No. 24, December 9, 2004, pp. 2471–2475.

Johnson, David E., and Gary Cecchine, *Conserving the Future Force Fighting Strength: Findings from the Army Medical Department Transformation Workshops, 2002*, Santa Monica, Calif.: RAND Corporation, MG-103-A, 2004.

———, *Medical Risk in the Future Force Unit of Action: Results of the Army Medical Department Transformation Workshop IV*, Santa Monica, Calif.: RAND Corporation, TR-253-A, 2005.

———, *Medical Risk in the Future Force Unit of Employment: Results of the Army Medical Department Transformation Workshop V*, Santa Monica, Calif.: RAND Corporation, TR-302-A, forthcoming.

Millot, Marc Dean, Roger C. Molander, and Peter Wilson, "*The Day After . . .*" *Study: Nuclear Proliferation in the Post–Cold War World, Volume I, Summary Report*, Santa Monica, Calif.: RAND Corporation, MR-266-AF, 1993.

Nechaev, E. A., A. J. Gritsanov, N. F. Fomin, and I. P. Minnullin, *Mine Blast Trauma: Experience from the War in Afghanistan*, St. Petersburg, Russia: Russian Ministry of Public Health and Medical Industry, 1995.

Patel, H. Tarak, Kimberly A. Wenner, Shaun A. Price, Michael A. Weber, Autumn Leverage, and Scott J. McAtee, "A U.S. Army Forward Surgical Team's Experience in Operation Iraqi Freedom," *Journal of Trauma Injury, Infection and Critical Care*, Vol. 57, No. 2, August 2004, pp. 201–207.

Trunkey, D. D., "Trauma," *Scientific American*, August 1983, Vol. 249, pp. 28–35.

U.S. Department of the Army, *DA Pam 40-19: Commander's Guide to Combat Health*, Washington, D.C.: Headquarters, Department of the Army, March 1995.

———, *FM 8-10-25: Employment of Forward Surgical Teams: Tactics, Techniques and Procedures*, Washington, D.C.: Headquarters, Department of the Army, 1997.

———, *FM 8-10-6: Medical Evacuation in a Theater of Operations: Tactics, Techniques and Procedures*, Washington, D.C.: Headquarters, Department of the Army, 2000a.

———, *Weapon Systems 2000*, Washington, D.C.: Headquarters, Department of the Army, 2000b, p. 256.

———, *FM 4-02.10: Theater Hospitalization*, Washington, D.C.: Headquarters, Department of the Army, January 2005.

U.S. Department of the Army, Training and Doctrine Command Analysis Center (TRAC), *Objective Force Concept Exploration: A Notional Combat Battalion Engagement*, TRAC F-TD-01-006, Washington, D.C.: Headquarters, Department of the Army, August 15, 2001.

Wright, Capt. H. D., and Capt. R. D. Harkness, *A Survey of Casualties Amongst Armored Units in Northwest Europe*, Medical Research Council Team, British Army Group (No. 2 ORS), January 1946.